Name: ....

Class: ....

School: ....

sh

Action
Place your finger over your lips and say *sh, sh, sh.*

am
get
clap
shop
fish
shut
wish
I
the
shampoo

Write an ‹sh› word in each fish and draw a picture to illustrate it.

Dictation

1.
2.
3.
4.
5.
6.
7.
8.
9.

Rainbow Capital Letters

Write a ‹ch› word in each chest and draw a picture to illustrate it.

Action
Move your arms as if you are a train and say *ch, ch, ch*.

if
hot
blot
chips
lunch
chest
much
he
she
chicken

Dictation

1.

2.

3.

4.

5.

6.

7.

8.

9.

Sentences

Put the words in the right order to make a sentence about the picture.

A

Put the words in the right order and colour the picture.

th

Action
Stick out your tongue, a little for th and further for *th*.

us
sad
flag
this
with
that
thank
me
we
thinking

Write a ‹th› word in each thought bubble and draw a picture.

thin

Dictation

1.

2.

3.

4.

5.

6.

7.

8.

9.

Are these sentences correct? Write out each sentence correctly on the line.

1. the dog is spotty.

2. The duck swims on the.

3. I sleep in a bunk bed.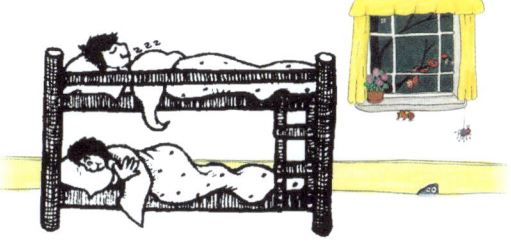

4. i like. fried eggs

5. They are playing ball.

ng

Action
Pretend to lift a heavy weight above your head and say *ng*.

in
leg
glad
ring
sang
strong
lung
be
was
length

Write an ‹ng› word in each ring and draw a picture to illustrate it.

- ang
- strength
- ing
- ong
- ung

Dictation

1.
2.
3.
4.
5.
6.
7.
8.
9.

Capital Letters

Write the capital letter next to each lower-case letter.

A a   b   c   d   e

   f   g   h   i   j

   k   l   m   n   o

   p   q   r   s   t

   u   v   w   x   y   z

Join each capital letter to the matching lower-case letter.

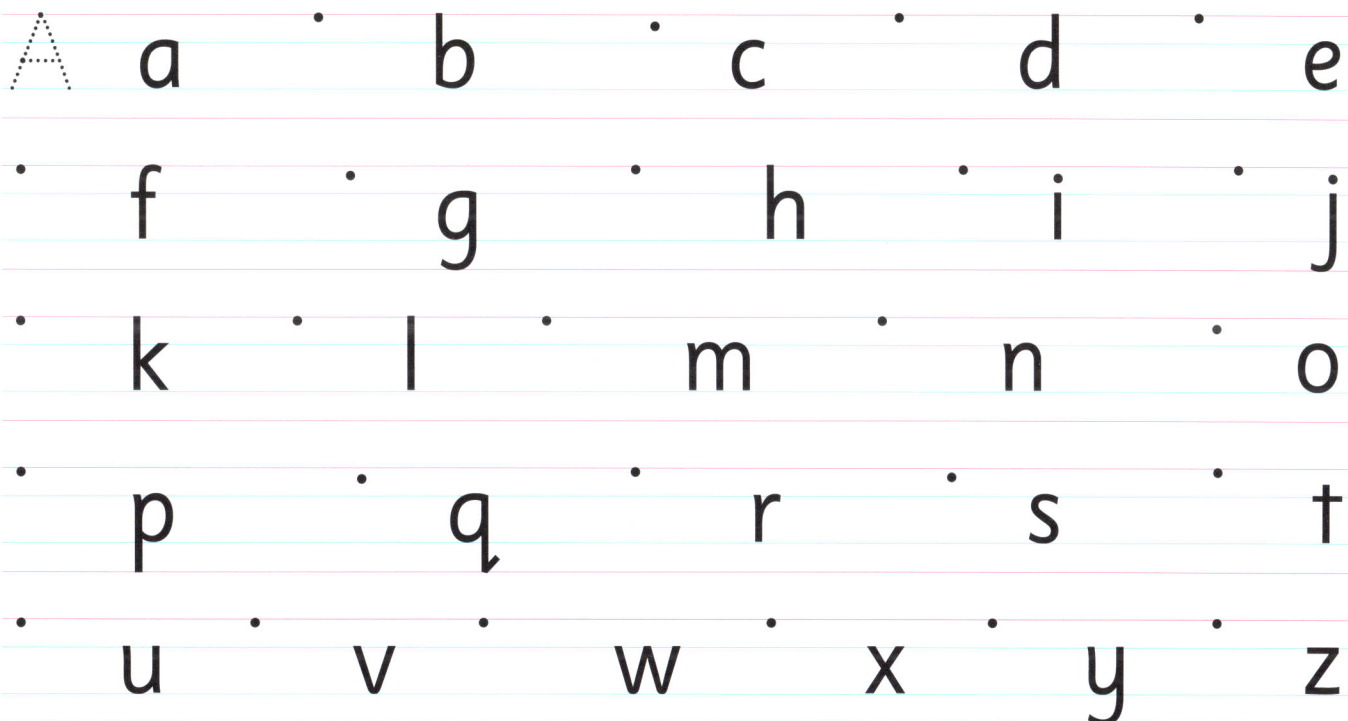

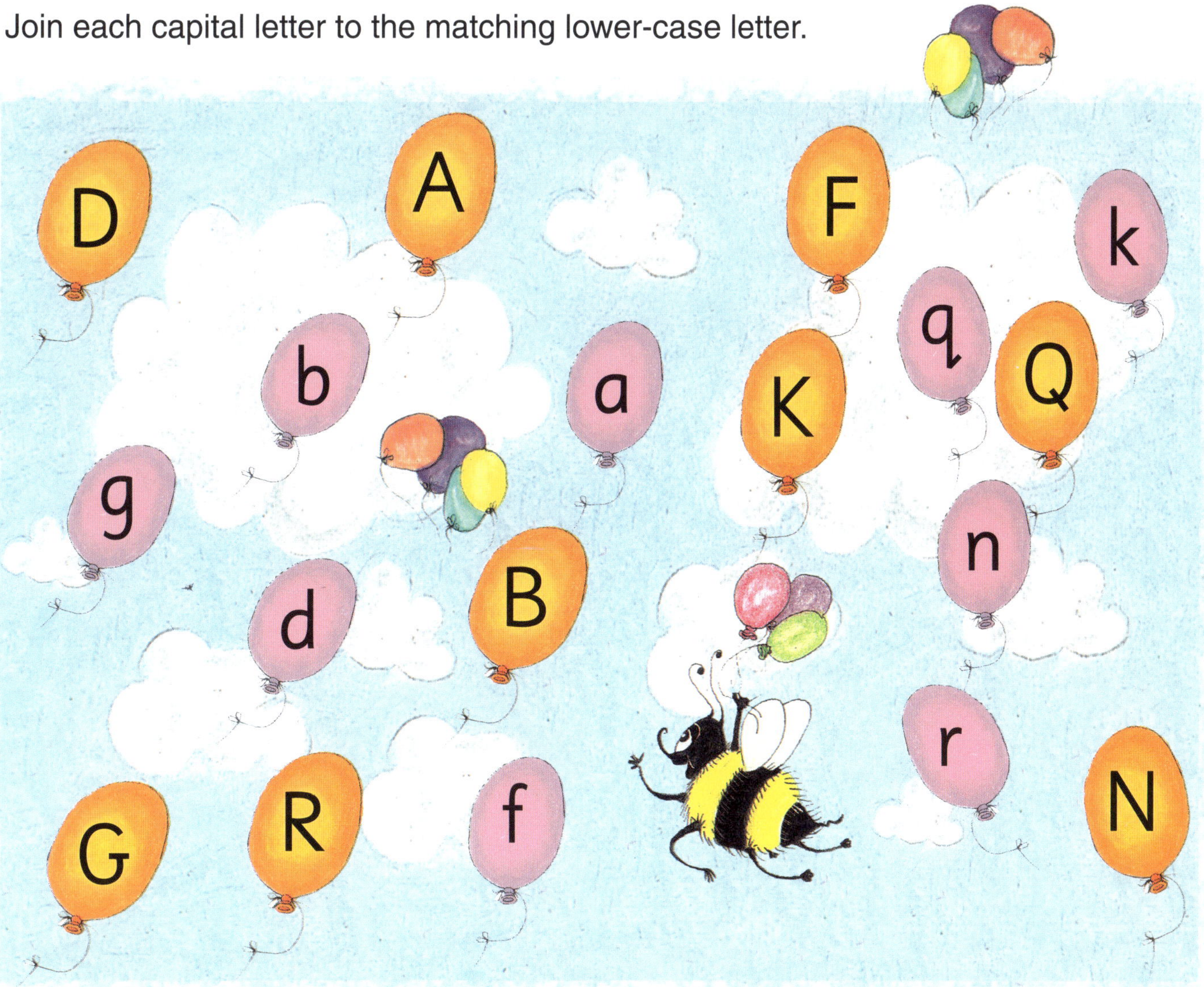

qu

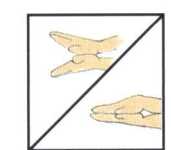

Action
Make a duck's beak with your hands and say *qu, qu, qu*.

on
but
plum
quick
quiz
queen
squid
to
do
squirrel

Write a ‹qu› word in each duck and draw a picture to illustrate it.

quack
qu

Dictation

1.

2.

3.

4.

5.

6.

7.

8.

9.

Proper Nouns

Action
Touch your forehead with your index and middle fingers.

Draw pictures of yourself and your teacher in the frames and write your names on the lines underneath.

Write your school's address on the envelope.

ar

Action
Open your mouth wide and say *ah*, as if at the doctors.

at
yes
slug
arm
hard
scarf
card
are
all
farmyard

Write an ‹ar› word in each star and draw a picture to illustrate it.

Dictation

1.

2.

3.

4.

5.

6.

7.

8.

9.

Action
Put your hand on your forehead.

Draw three pictures and write the nouns underneath.

Write a noun in the gap to finish each sentence and draw its picture in the box.

1. The _____ is black.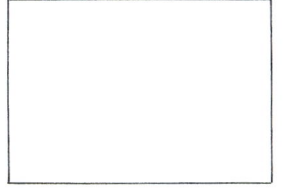

2. I throw the _____ .

3. A _____ can swim.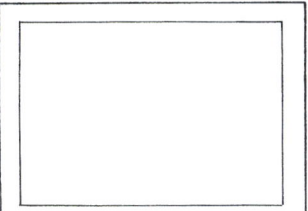

4. I like to eat _____ .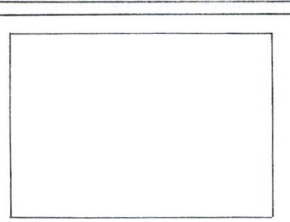

Fill each container with short vowel words. Write /a/ words in the bag, /e/ words in the net, /i/ words in the bin, /o/ words in the box and /u/ words in the mug.

Vowel Hand

dog
bran
Monday
Tuesday
Wednesday
Thursday
Friday
you
your
Saturday

Dictation

1.

2.

3.

4.

5.

6.

7.

8.

9.

Write an ‹ff› word in each cliff and draw a picture to illustrate it.

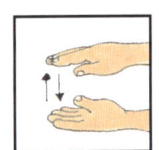

Action
Bring your hands together gently and say ffffffff.

up
man
crab
off
cliff
stiff
cuff
come
some
stuffing

Dictation

1.

2.

3.

4.

5.

6.

7.

8.

9.

a or an?

Write '**an**' before each word beginning with a vowel and write '**a**' before each word beginning with a consonant.

 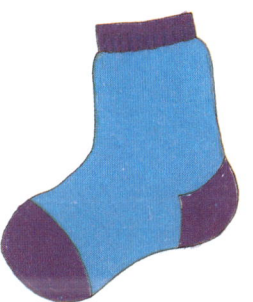 

A a E e I i O o U u

ll

Action
Pretend to lick a lollipop and say *l, l, l.*

red
win
drum
will
bell
doll
skull
said
here
windmill

Write an ‹ll› word in each bell and draw a picture to illustrate it.

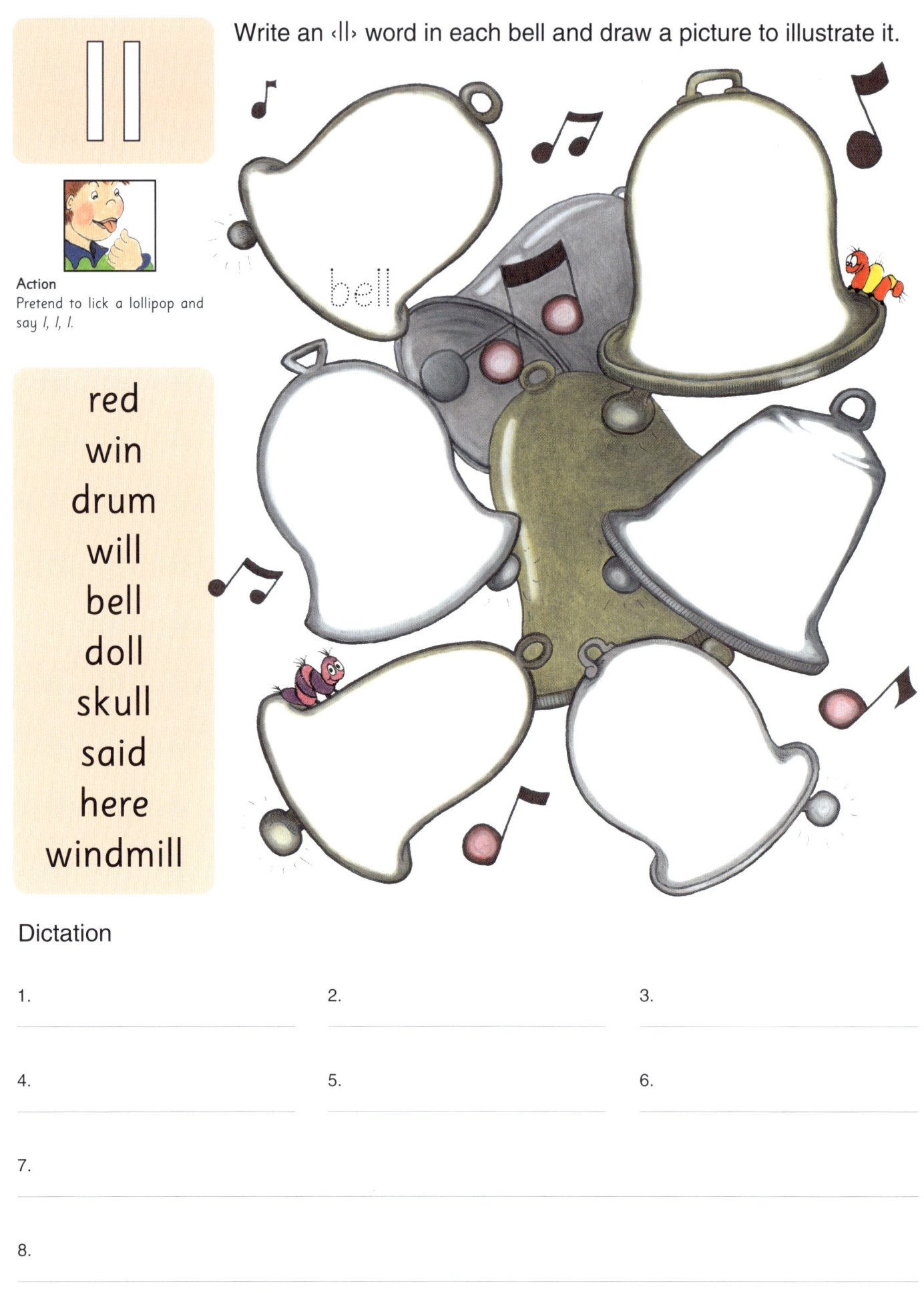

Dictation

1.

2.

3.

4.

5.

6.

7.

8.

9.

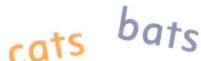

cats bats rats

Plurals

socks dots books

Illustrate each word in the boxes.

hats	pens	dog
cars	cow	frog

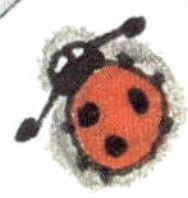

Write the word for each picture.

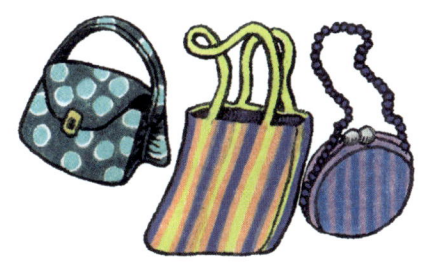

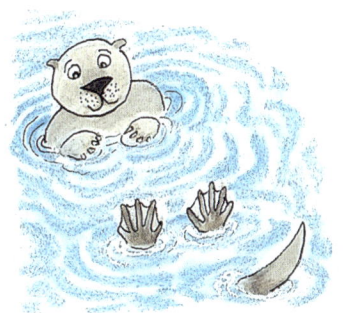

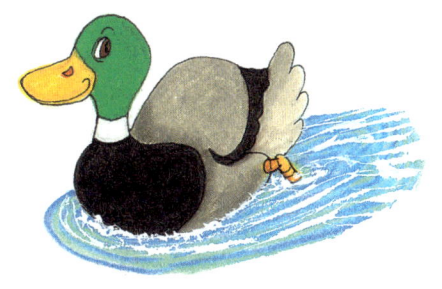

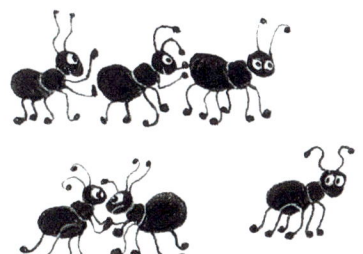

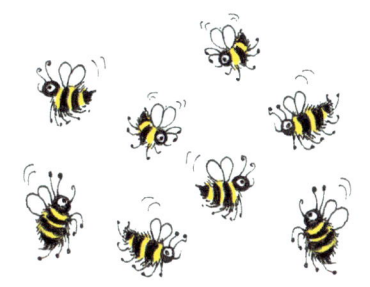

ss zz

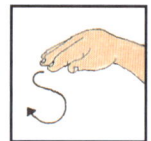

Action Weave your hand in an ‹s› shape, saying sssss.

Action Put your arms out like a bee's wings, and say zzzzzz.

Write an ‹ss› word in each dress and a ‹zz› word in the bee. Draw a picture for each word.

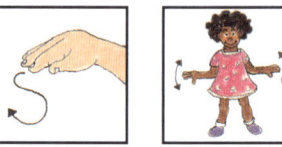

ox
run
from
buzz
cross
less
miss
there
they
crossroads

Dictation

1.

2.

3.

4.

5.

6.

7.

8.

9.

Draw a picture for each pronoun.
Remember to draw more than one person for the plural pronouns.

Singular Pronouns

Singular Pronouns

I

Point to yourself.

you

Point to someone else.

he

Point to a boy.

she

Point to a girl.

it

Point to the floor.

Plural Pronouns

we

Point in a circle to include yourself and others.

you

Point to two other people.

they

Point to the next-door class.

Plural Pronouns

21

ck

Action
Snap your fingers together, saying ck, ck, ck.

hop
fit
grin
duck
neck
clock
lick
go
no
broomstick

Write a ‹ck› word in each chick and draw a picture to illustrate it.

Dictation

1.

2.

3.

4.

5.

6.

7.

8.

9.

Initial Consonant Blends

Read the initial consonant blends around the edge of the page and trace inside them. Use these blends to make a word in each box. Draw a picture to illustrate your word.

fr   dr   cr   sm

sk   gr

sp   sl

gl   fl

st   bl

sw   cl   tr   sn

slug   __og   __ab

__ub   __in   __ee

__ing   __ape   __ider

y

Action
Put your hands on your head like donkey's ears and say *ee*.

bed
wet
prod
holly
party
story
happy
so
my
family

Write a word with ‹y› at the end in each holly leaf and draw a picture.

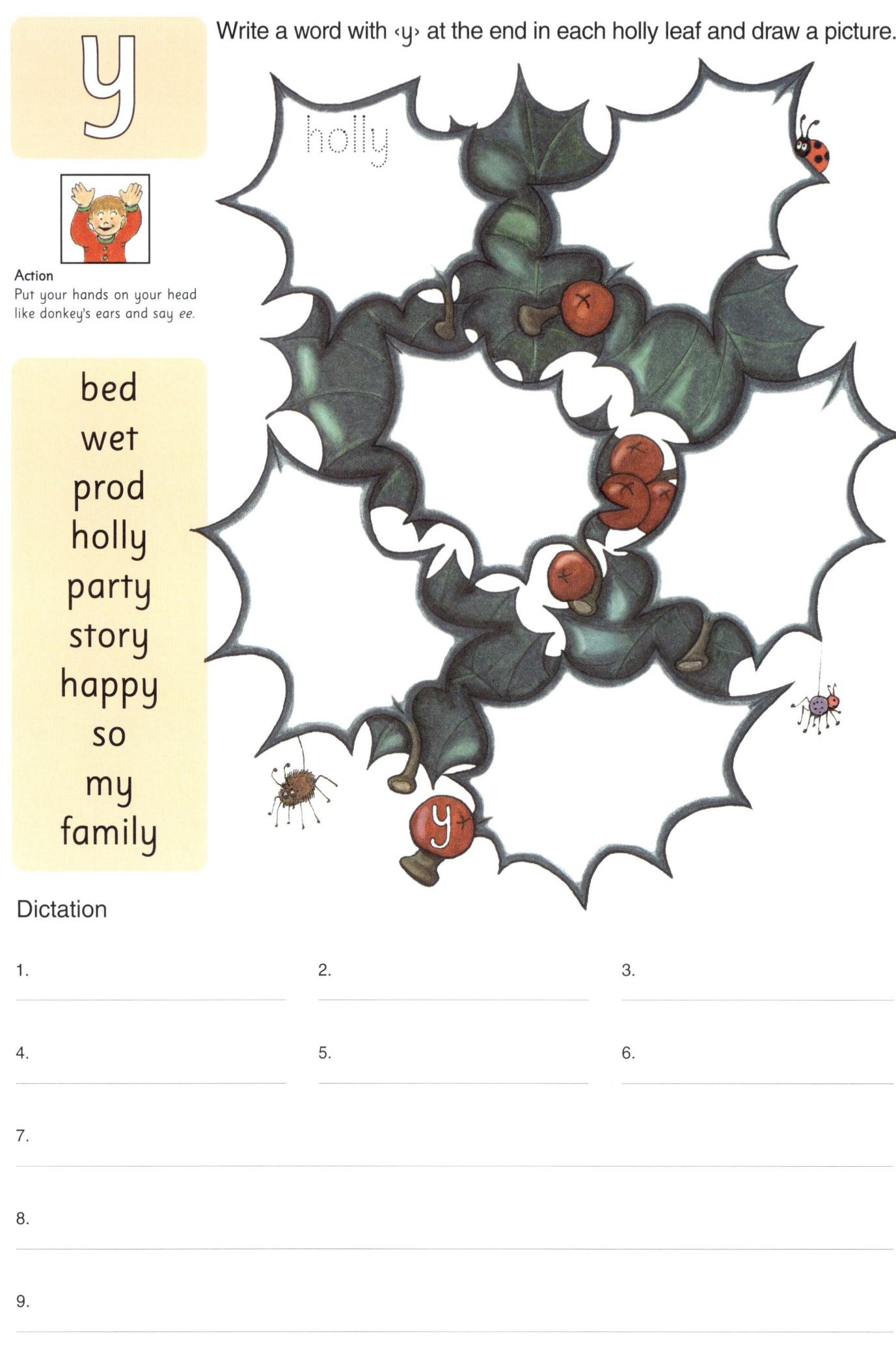

Dictation

1.

2.

3.

4.

5.

6.

7.

8.

9.

Initial Consonant Blends

Write the word underneath each picture. All the words have initial consonant blends.

Read the words in the leaves. If the word has a short vowel sound, colour the leaf's edge yellow.

a e i
o u

sad
let
trip
blue
orange
grey
black
one
by
colour

cake, hum, fig, sky, nut, toe, ride, week, tie, way, home, reed, fox, tune, soap, cod, map, yam, bit, wet, tug, fez, toad

Dictation

1.

2.

3.

4.

5.

6.

7.

8.

9.

Alphabetical Order

When looking up words in a dictionary, it helps to think of the alphabet in sections.
Trace inside each capital letter using a different colour for each section of the alphabet.
Write the lower-case letters next to the capital letters.

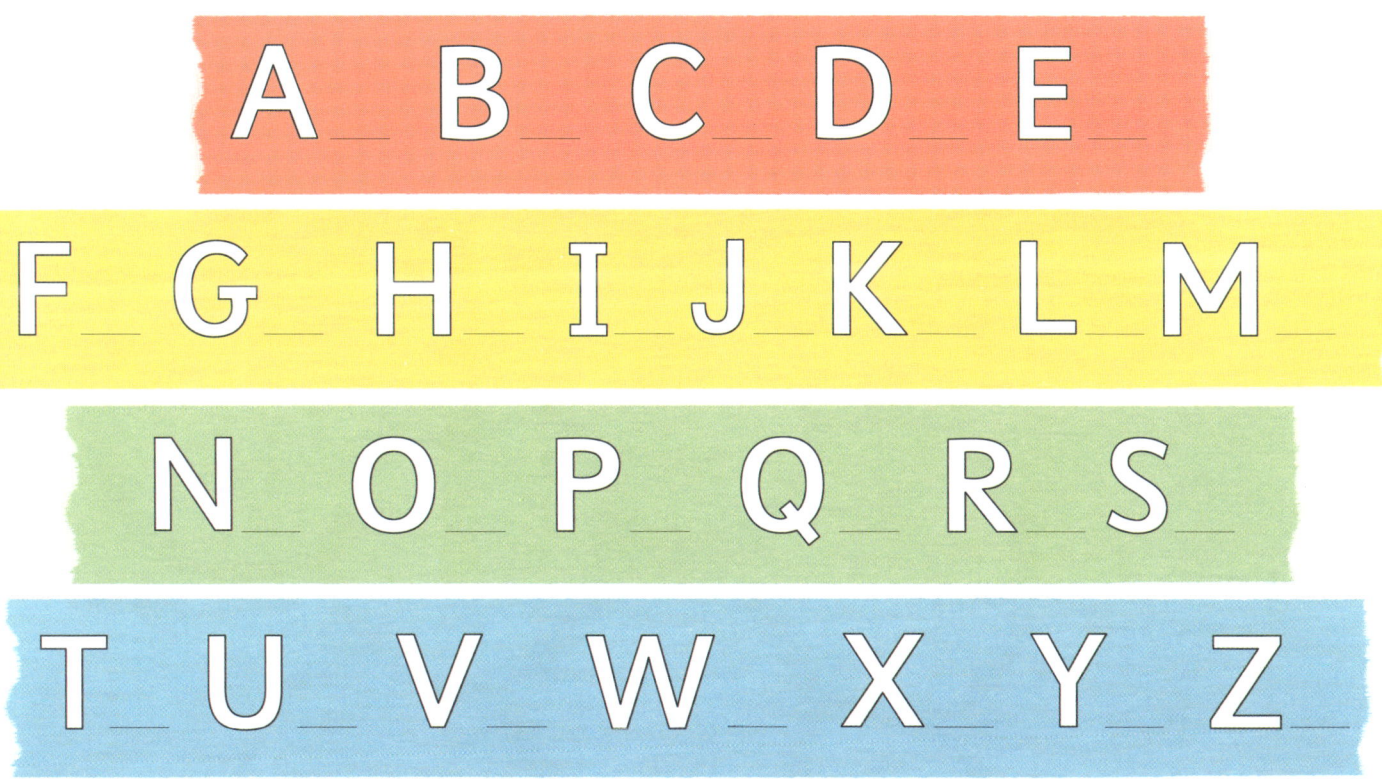

Dictionaries tell you how a word is spelt and what it means.
Find each letter in the dictionary and write down the first word beginning with that letter.

A a _____   G g _____

N n _____   O o _____

S s _____   Z z _____

Put these sets of letters into alphabetical order.

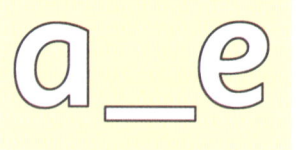

Action
Cup your hand over your ear and say *ai, ai, ai.*

Add ‹a_e› to make a word in each grape. Read and illustrate each word.

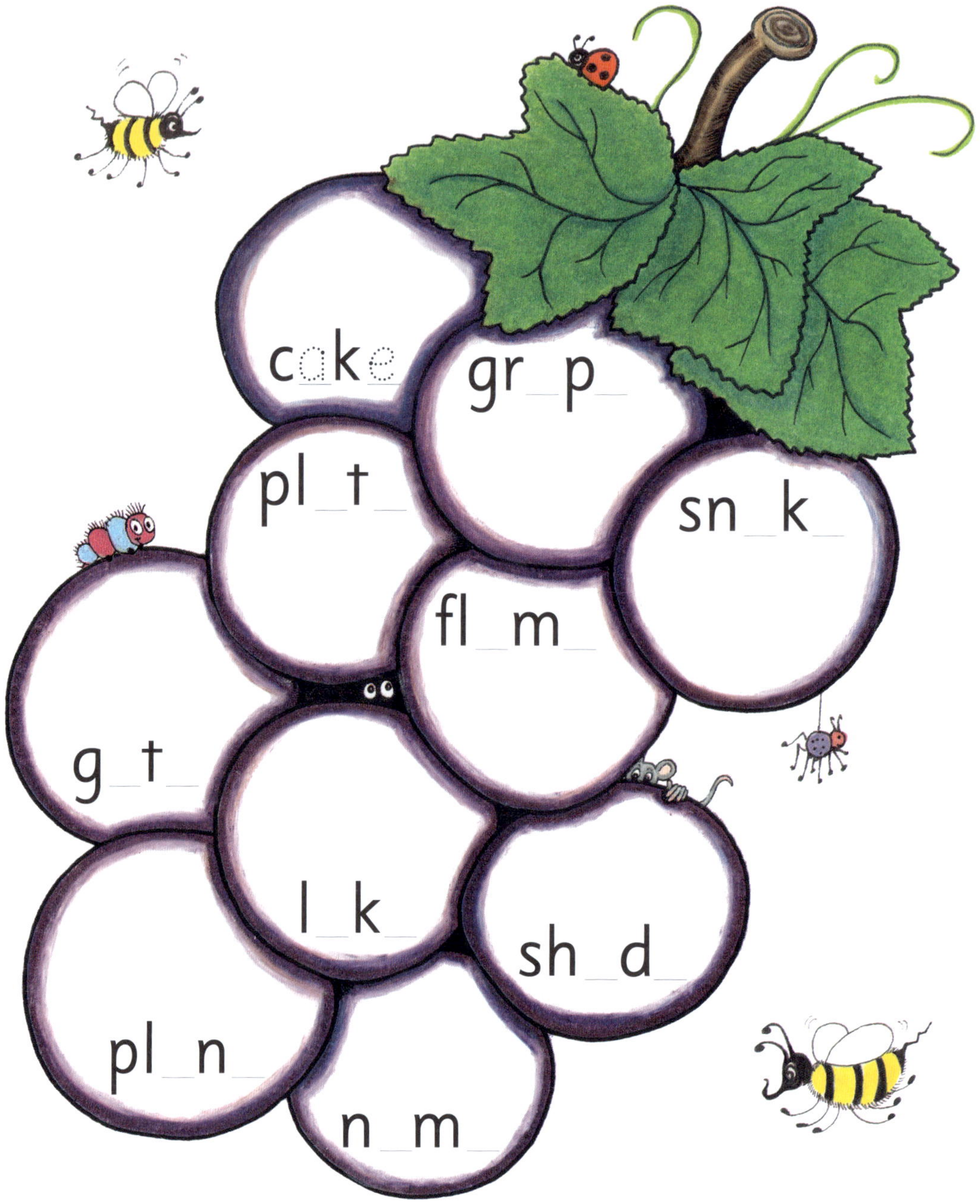

cake
gr_p_
pl_t_
sn_k_
fl_m_
g_t_
l_k_
sh_d_
pl_n_
n_m_

ran
hat
scar
came
grape
name
cake
only
old
baseball

Dictation

1.

2.

3.

4.

5.

6.

7.

8.

9.

Verbs

Action
Move your arms back and forth at your sides, as if you are running.

Write the verb underneath each picture.

      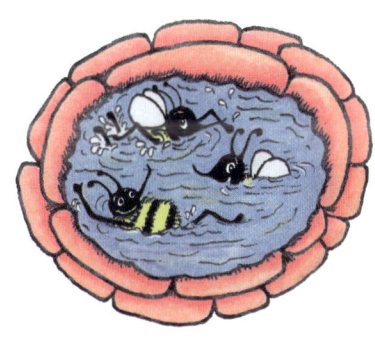

to _____   to _____   to _____

Draw a bee doing each verb.

      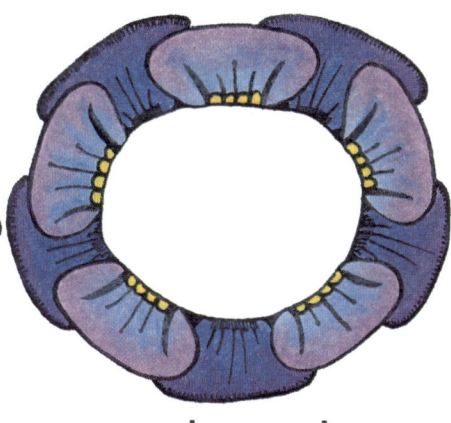

to cry   to hop   to brush

Think of three more verbs and illustrate them in the flowers.

to _____   to _____   to _____

i_e

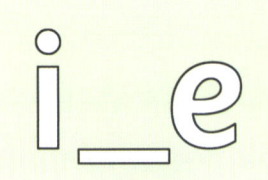

Action
Stand to attention and salute, saying *ie, ie*.

six
pad
smell
bike
time
smile
prize
like
have
bridesmaid

Add ‹i_e› to make a word in each kite. Read and illustrate each word.

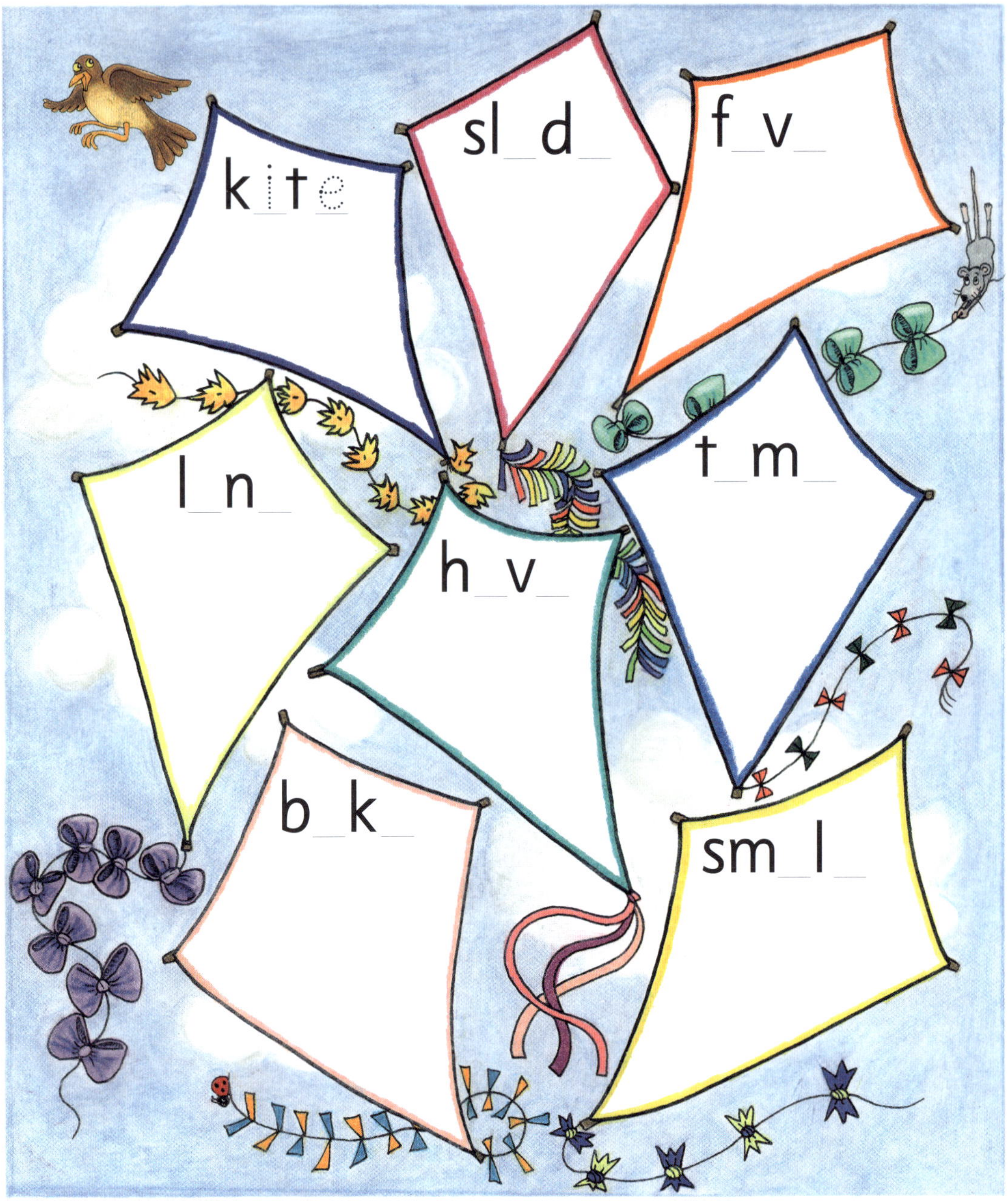

kite   sl_d_   f_v_
l_n_   t_m_
h_v_
b_k_   sm_l_

Dictation

1.

2.

3.

4.

5.

6.

7.

8.

9.

Verbs

Think of a verb and write it on the line.

to _____

Write the verb next to each pronoun, and draw a picture for each person doing the verb. Remember that the verb has an ‹s› at the end when joined to the third person singular, and that you must draw more than one person for the plural pronouns.

1st person singular   2nd person singular   3rd person singular

I _____   you _____   he
she _____
it

1st person plural   2nd person plural   3rd person plural

we _____   you _____   they _____

31

o_e

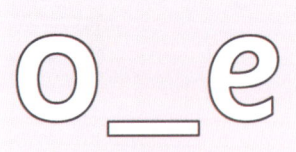

Action
Bring your hand over your mouth and say *oh!*

cod
lot
snap
bone
nose
home
globe
live
give
tadpole

Add ‹o_e› to make a word in each tadpole. Illustrate each word.

Dictation

1.

2.

3.

4.

5.

6.

7.

8.

9.

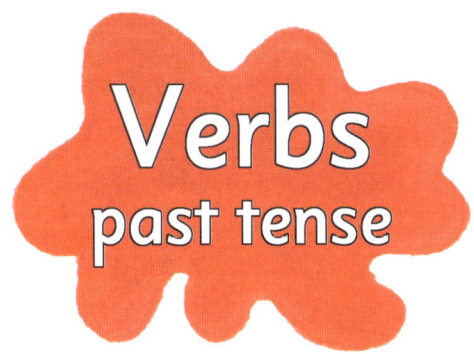

Verbs past tense

Present Tense Action 	Past Tense Action 
Point towards the floor with the palm of your hand.	Point backwards over your shoulder with your thumb.

The simplest way to make the past tense is by adding ‹ed› to the verb.

Today, I **talk**. talk + ed Yesterday, I **talked**.

If a verb already ends with an ‹e›, cross it off before adding ‹ed›.

Today, I **smile**. smil̶e + ed Yesterday, I **smiled**.

Put these verbs into the past tense.

Present	Past	Present	Past
jump	_____	hope	_____
paint	_____	play	_____
like	_____	wave	_____
shout	_____	skate	_____
rest	_____	twist	_____

Underline the verbs in red.
Then decide whether the sentences are in the present or the past.

She brushed her hair.   (past) / present

They look out of the window.   past / present

I cooked dinner.   past / present

The race started in the park.   past / present

u_e

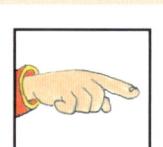

Action
Point at people around you and say *you, you, you*.

bus
pot
swim
cube
tune
used
excuse
little
down
useless

Add ‹u_e› to make a word in each musical note. Illustrate each word.

tune
m_l_
t_b_
c_b_
d_k_

Dictation

1.
2.
3.
4.
5.
6.
7.
8.
9.

Verbs

hoped

hopped

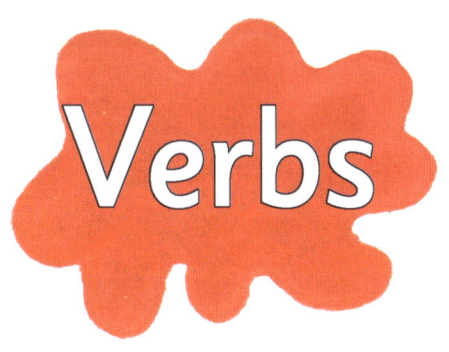

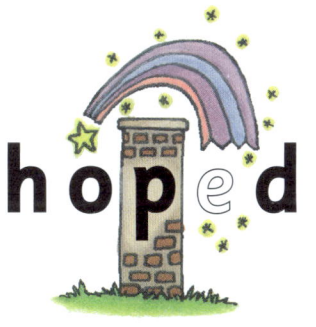

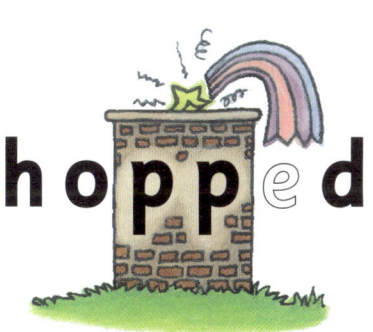

Write these verbs in the simple past tense.

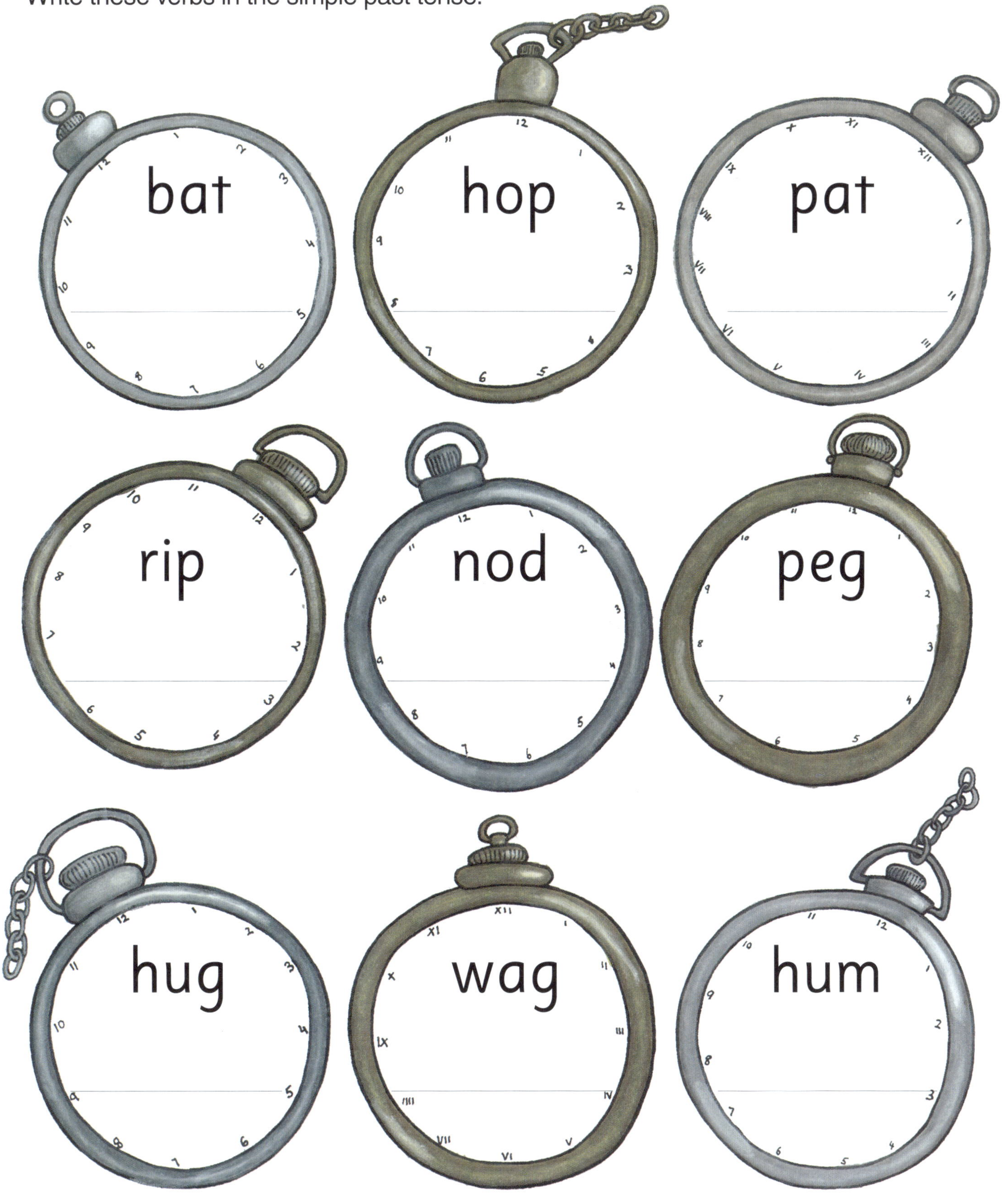
bat
hop
pat
rip
nod
peg
hug
wag
hum

wh

Action
Blow onto your open hands and say *wh, wh, wh*.

did
cut
twin
whale
wheel
white
whisper
what
when
whenever

Write a ‹wh› word in each whale and draw a picture to illustrate it.

whale

Dictation

1.
2.
3.
4.
5.
6.
7.
8.
9.

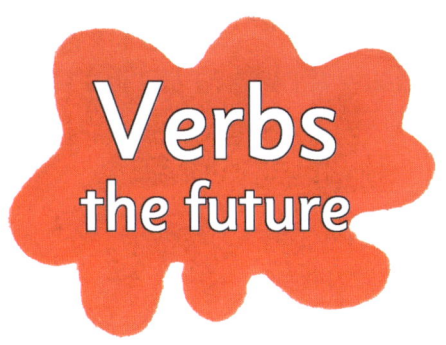

Action
Point to the front.

Read the verbs in the *today* column. Then write the verbs in the past tense in the *yesterday* column, and in the future in the *tomorrow* column.

Past yesterday	Present today	Future tomorrow
I talked	I talk	I shall talk
I _____	I cook	I _____
I _____	I listen	I _____
I _____	I skate	I _____
I _____	I walk	I _____

Write some sentences about what you did yesterday.

_____

_____

Write some sentences about what you will do tomorrow.

_____

_____

ay

Write an ‹ay› word in each crayon and draw a picture to illustrate it.

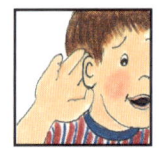

Action
Cup your hand over your ear and say *ai, ai, ai*.

an
cat
skin
say
away
play
today
why
where
playground

Dictation

1.

2.

3.

4.

5.

6.

7.

8.

9.

Alphabetical Order

Write the capital letters next to the lower-case letters.

__ a __ b __ c __ d __ e

__ f __ g __ h __ i __ j __ k __ l __ m

__ n __ o __ p __ q __ r __ s

__ t __ u __ v __ w __ x __ y __ z

Put these sets of letters into alphabetical order.

F ___
B ___
X ___
O ___

T ___
C ___
N ___
H ___

q ___
w ___
i ___
r ___

Put these sets of words into alphabetical order.

Inky
Snake
Bee

pear
apple
orange

Action
Put your hands on your head like donkey's ears and say *ee*.

Write an ‹ea› word in each teapot and draw a picture to illustrate it.

met
web
spin
tea
heat
leaf
each
who
which
seashell

Dictation

1.

2.

3.

4.

5.

6.

7.

8.

9.

Nouns

Write six nouns for the things you can see in the picture.

a _____ the _____

a _____ the _____

a _____ the _____

Underline the nouns in black. There can be more than one noun in a sentence.

1. The cow is black and white.
2. Jim drives a red and yellow tractor.
3. The sheep graze on the hills.
4. On Andrew's farm, there are cows, sheep, chickens and a horse.

igh

Action
Stand to attention and salute, saying *ie, ie*.

lip
his
went
night
high
might
light
any
many
frightening

Write an ‹igh› word in each light bulb and draw a picture.

Dictation

1.

2.

3.

4.

5.

6.

7.

8.

9.

Adjectives

Action
Touch the side of your temple with your fist.

Colour the snakes so that they match the adjectives.

You can use more than one adjective at a time.
Colour the snake to make it fit your description.

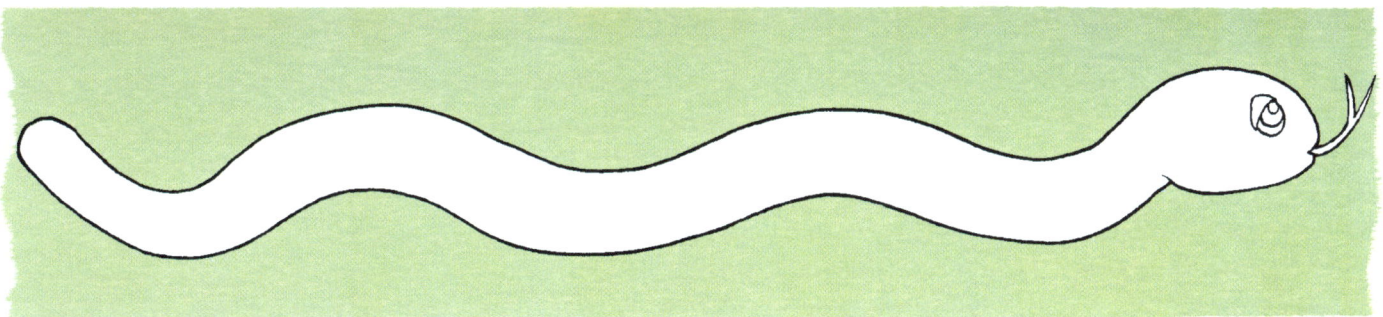

a _____, _____, _____ snake

y

Action
Stand to attention and salute, saying *ie, ie*.

win
sit
stop
fry
dry
crying
sky
more
before
myself

Write a ‹y› word in each frying pan and draw a picture to illustrate it.

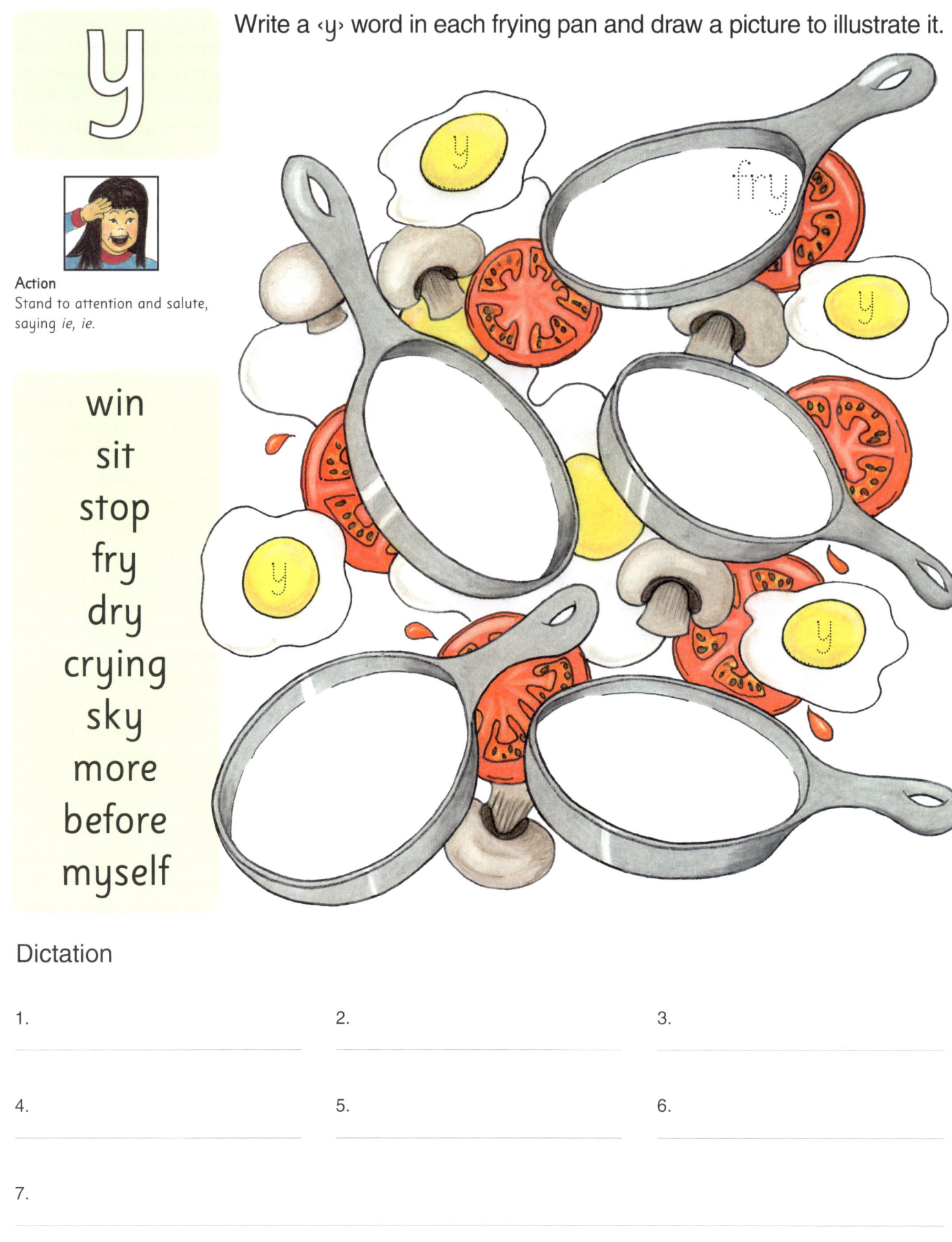

Dictation

1.

2.

3.

4.

5.

6.

7.

8.

9.

Adjectives

Underline the nouns in black. Find an adjective to describe each noun. There are some adjectives in the snake to help you.

A _____ snake hisses.

My _____ shirt is new.

The _____ dog barks.

Her _____ car stopped.

The sky is _____.

The tree is _____.

The _____ flowers smell.

The film was _____.

His _____ balloon burst.

My coat is _____ and _____.

Write an ‹ow› word in each snowman and draw a picture to illustrate it.

Action
Bring your hand over your mouth and say *oh!*

box
job
bulb
own
grow
elbow
yellow
other
were
snowman

Dictation

1.

2.

3.

4.

5.

6.

7.

8.

9.

Final Consonant Blends

Read the final consonant blends at the top of the page and trace inside them. Use these blends to make a word in each box. Draw a picture to illustrate your word.

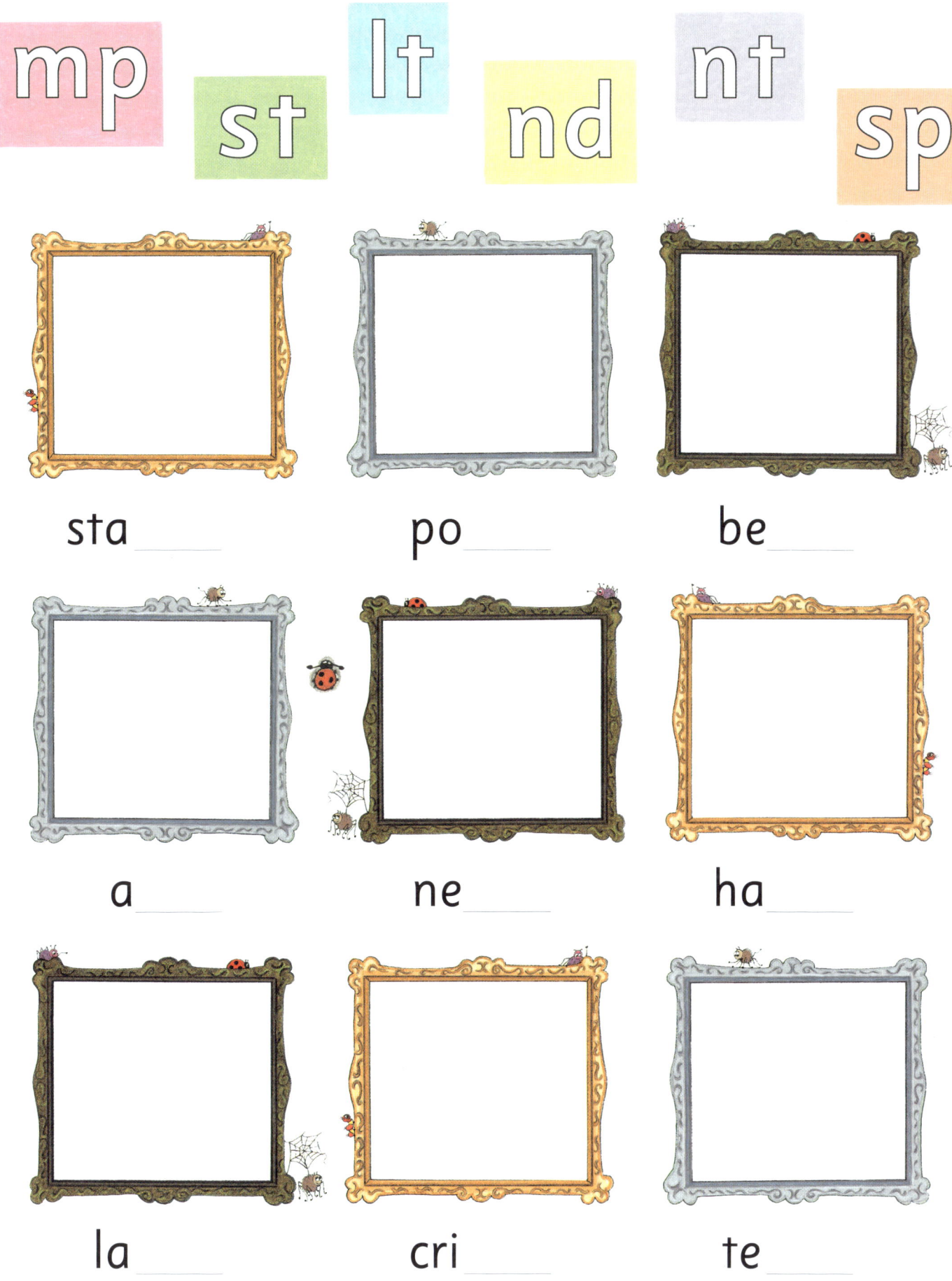

Write an ‹ew› word in each jewel and draw a picture to illustrate it.

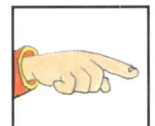

Action
Point at people around you and say *you, you, you.*

Action
Move your head forward and say *oo.*

bud
sun
held
few
flew
grew
chew
because
want
newspaper

jewel

Dictation

1.

2.

3.

4.

5.

6.

7.

8.

9.

Compound Words

The compound word birds have muddled up their tails. Can you sort them out? Colour the tails to match the bodies.

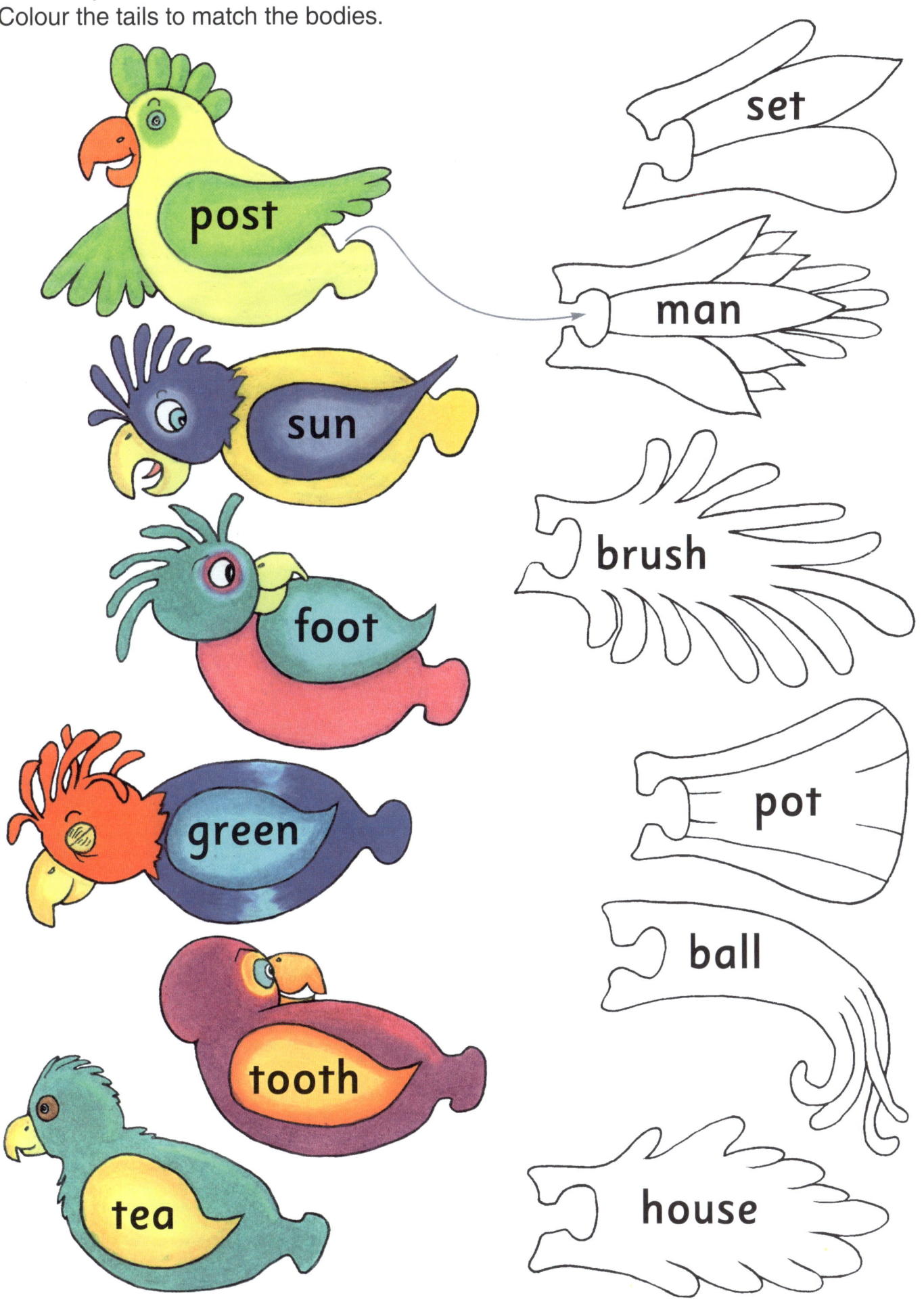

ou

Write an ‹ou› word in each house and draw a picture to illustrate it.

Action
Pretend your finger is a needle and prick your thumb, saying ou, ou, ou.

bat
pet
self
out
our
round
mouth
saw
put
outside

house

Dictation

1.

2.

3.

4.

5.

6.

7.

8.

9.

Alphabetical Order

Put these sets of words into alphabetical order.

1. car   tractor   lorry

   a._____ b._____ c._____

2. hamster   cat   rabbit

   a._____ b._____ c._____

3. lemon   apple   banana

   a._____ b._____ c._____

4. Sam   Alex   Ravi   Gilbert

   a._____ b._____ c._____ d._____

5. Emily   Pat   Davinda   Sue   Jill

   a._____ b._____ c._____ d._____ e._____

ABCDEFGHIJKLMNOPQRSTUVWXYZ

Look up the words for these nouns in your dictionary. Carefully copy out the words.

Write an ‹ow› word in each owl and draw a picture to illustrate it.

Action
Pretend your finger is a needle and prick your thumb, saying ou, ou, ou.

big
fox
milk
how
owl
brown
town
could
should
flowerpot

owl

Dictation

1.

2.

3.

4.

5.

6.

7.

8.

9.

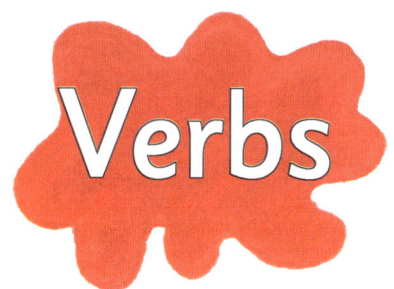

Verbs

Write six verbs for the actions you can see in the picture.

to _____   to _____

to _____   to _____

to _____   to _____

Underline the verbs in red. There can be more than one verb in a sentence.

1. Jenny smiled at her friend.

2. Alex sails a boat.

3. Hannah swims and dives in the sea.

4. The boys make a sand castle and then play football.

oi

Action
Cup your hands around your mouth and shout *oi, ship ahoy!*

Write an ‹oi› word in each oil can and draw a picture to illustrate it.

bug
had
film
oil
coin
noisy
toil
would
right
boiling

Dictation

1.

2.

3.

4.

5.

6.

7.

8.

9.

Adverbs

Action
Bang one fist on top of the other.

Choose an adverb to go with each picture.

quickly   hungrily   slowly

secretly   happily   loudly

Inky eats _____.

Snake slithers _____.

Bee buzzes _____.

The ants whisper _____.

The snail goes _____.

The band played _____.

oy

Write an ‹oy› word in each toy and draw a picture to illustrate it.

Action
Cup your hands around your mouth and shout *oi, ship ahoy!*

jet
dig
help
boy
toy
enjoy
annoy
two
four
destroy

Dictation

1.

2.

3.

4.

5.

6.

7.

8.

9.

Adverbs

Read the adverbs below, then read the story in the beehive. Write an adverb in each space.

loudly   soon   suddenly

happily   quickly   slowly

Bee's Busy Day

Bee woke up _____, and traipsed _____ down the hive to have breakfast. She buzzed _____ as she flew to the farm. She _____ collected as much pollen as she could, and flew _____ back to the hive. She smiled _____ to herself. Bee, and her friends Inky and Snake, had planned a day out.

or

Action
Put your hands on your head pointing down, like donkey's ears, and say *or*.

got
bun
belt
fork
storm
horse
forty
goes
does
morning

Write an ‹or› word in each horse and draw a picture to illustrate it.

Dictation

1.

2.

3.

4.

5.

6.

7.

8.

9.

es es es es es es

Plurals ‹es›

In the first column, write a noun ending in ‹sh›, ‹ch›, ‹s› or ‹x› and draw a picture.
Write the plural of each noun in the second column.

sh

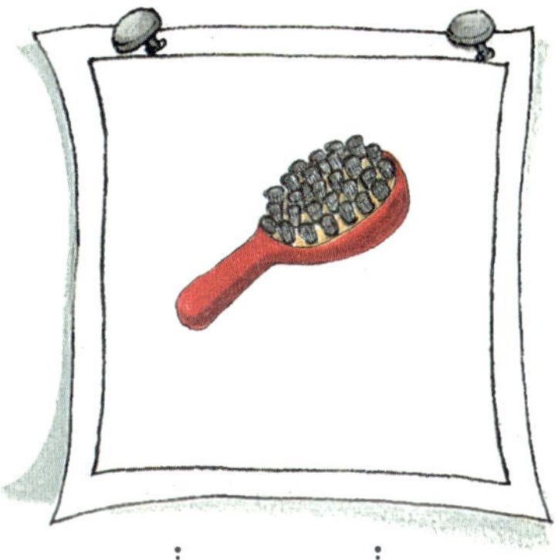

brush

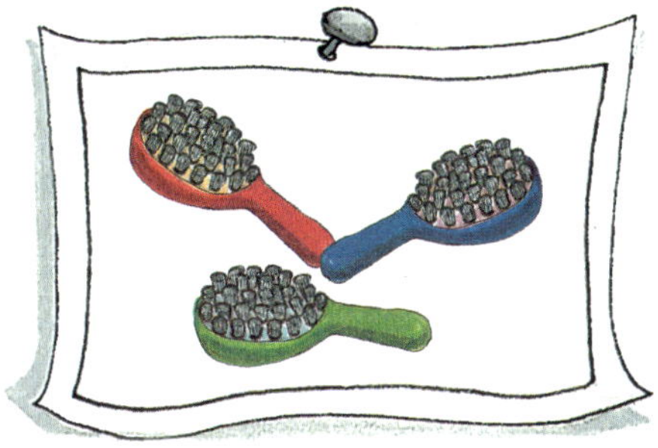

brushes

ch

s

x

al

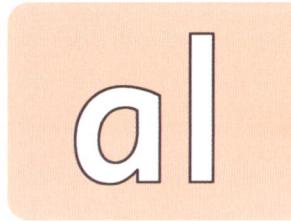

Action
Put your hands on your head pointing down, like donkey's ears, and say *or*.

bad
vet
fact
all
talk
walk
small
made
their
beanstalk

Write an ‹al› word in each bubble and draw a picture to illustrate it.

talk

Dictation

1.

2.

3.

4.

5.

6.

7.

8.

9.

Opposites   Antonyms

Write each opposite and draw a picture.

nk

Write an ‹nk› word in each drink and draw a picture to illustrate it.

Action
Pretend to lift a heavy weight above your head and say *ng*.

Action
Snap your fingers together, saying *ck, ck, ck*.

fin
sob
left
sink
pink
drink
think
once
upon
winking

Dictation

1.

2.

3.

4.

5.

6.

7.

8.

9.

Using a Dictionary

We can use a dictionary to check how to spell words.
Look up each word in your dictionary to circle the right spelling.

toofbrush   rabbit   starr
toothbrush   rabit   star

octopus   flouer   buterfie
octapus   flower   butterfly

These words are spelt incorrectly. Look them up and copy out the correct spelling.

boock   **carpit**   **triangel**

_____   _____   _____

We can also use a dictionary to find out what a word means.
Look up these words and write down their meanings.

atlas _____

yacht _____

Action
Roll your hands over each other like a mixer, saying ererererer.

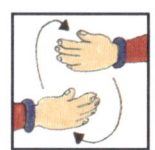

mud
jam
sent
term
summer
river
number
always
also
woodpecker

Write an ‹er› word in each ginger biscuit and draw a picture.

term

Dictation

1.

2.

3.

4.

5.

6.

7.

8.

9.

"Speech Marks"

“ ” “ ” “ ” “ ” “ ”

What are these animals saying?
Write their speech inside the speech bubbles, and then in between speech marks.

“ ” “ ” “

said the bee.　　said the snake.　　said the bird.

” ” ”

said the cow.　　said the donkey.　　said the duck.

ir

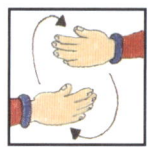

Action
Roll your hands over each other like a mixer, saying *ererererer*.

yet
hid
wept
skirt
girl
shirt
first
of
eight
birthday

Write an ‹ir› word in each bird and draw a picture to illustrate it.

Dictation

1.

2.

3.

4.

5.

6.

7.

8.

9.

Word Web

How many words could you use instead of *said*? Write the words in the word web.

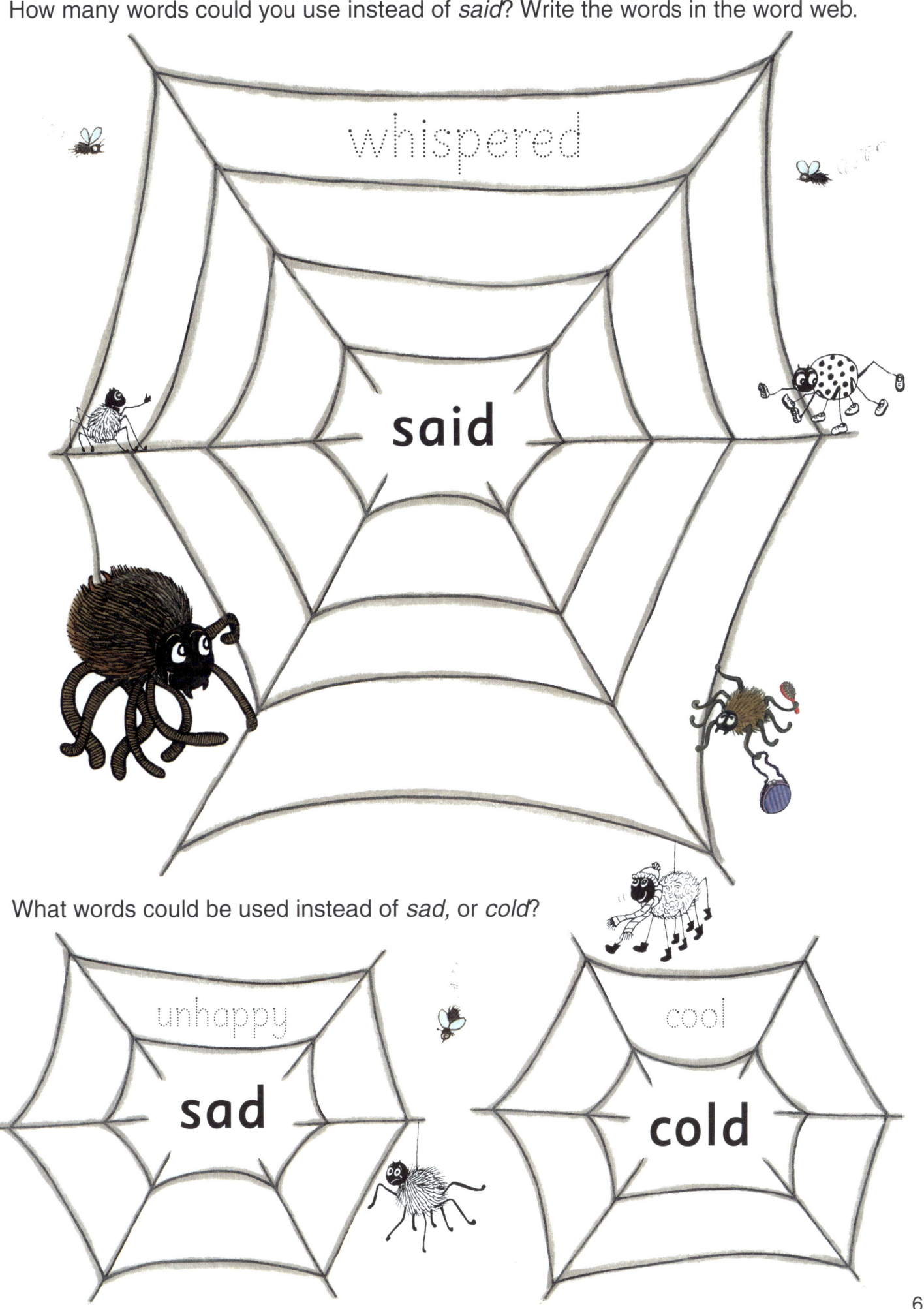

What words could be used instead of *sad*, or *cold*?

ur

Action
Roll your hands over each other like a mixer, saying *ererererer*.

Write a ‹ur› word in each turkey and draw a picture to illustrate it.

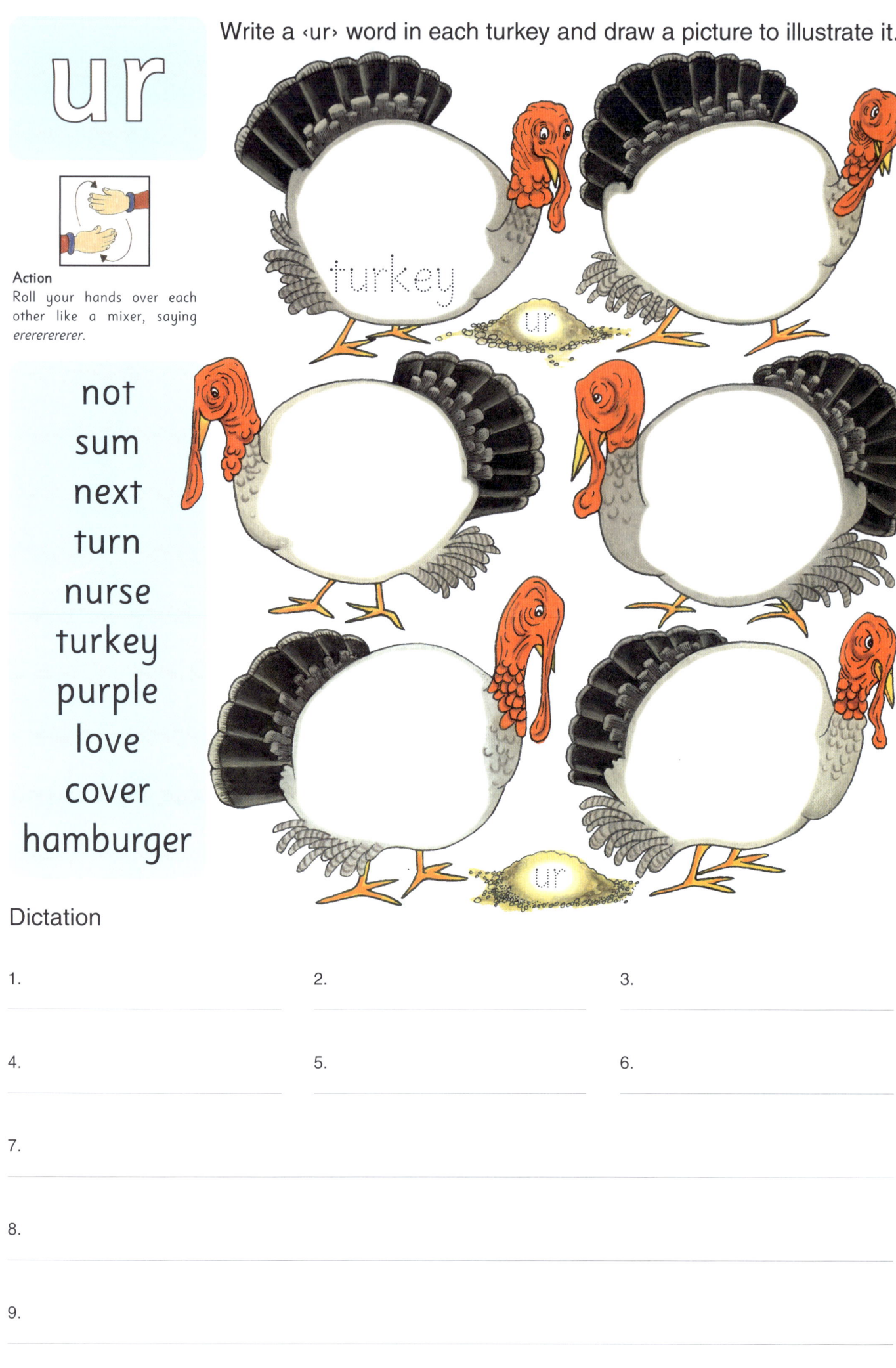

not
sum
next
turn
nurse
turkey
purple
love
cover
hamburger

Dictation

1.

2.

3.

4.

5.

6.

7.

8.

9.

Questions

We use these words to ask questions.

 what   why   when
where   who   which

Trace inside the question marks, using different colours.

Answer these questions.

1. What is your name? _____

2. Where do you live? _____

3. When is your birthday? _____

If you met someone for the first time, what questions would you ask them?

_____

_____

_____

_____

au

Action
Put your hands on your head pointing down, like donkey's ears, and say *or*.

map
fix
jump
fault
pause
haunt
August
after
every
astronaut

Write an ‹au› word in each astronaut and draw a picture.

Dictation

1.

2.

3.

4.

5.

6.

7.

8.

9.

Questions

You ask questions to find things out.

what where when why who which

Choose a question word to fit each sentence.

1. _____ won the quiz?

2. _____ time is it?

3. _____ book do you like best?

4. _____ are you going on holiday?

5. _____ did you do that?

6. _____ can we play tennis?

Read the questions and answers and see if you can guess which animal the girl is thinking of.

1. Do you have fur? Yes
2. How many legs do you have? Four
3. Do you have long ears? Yes
4. What do you eat? Carrots, oats and grass

Which animal is it?

Find a partner and play the game yourself.

aw

Write an ‹aw› word in each saw and draw a picture to illustrate it.

Action
Put your hands on your head pointing down, like donkey's ears, and say *or*.

zip
men
pond
saw
claw
dawn
prawn
mother
father
strawberry

Dictation

1.

2.

3.

4.

5.

6.

7.

8.

9.

Read the story below. Then underline the nouns in black and the verbs in red.

 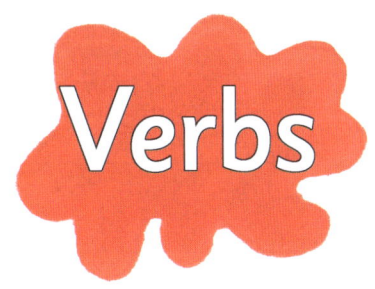

Inky toils long and hard in the garden. She digs the brown earth. The birds watch her interestedly. They wait eagerly for the grubs.

In the spring, Inky plants the seeds in the ground. She grows orange carrots, crispy lettuces and tall, green beans. In summer, she carefully harvests the yummy vegetables and eats them.

Inky also grows tall, yellow sunflowers in the garden. She likes the lovely sunflowers. The birds also like the sunflowers. They hungrily eat the striped black and white seeds.

Now see if you can underline the pronouns in pink, the adjectives in blue and the adverbs in orange.

Spellings

Spelling Test 1

1.
2.
3.
4.
5.
6.
7.
8.
9.
10.

Spelling Test 2

1.
2.
3.
4.
5.
6.
7.
8.
9.
10.

Spelling Test 3

1.
2.
3.
4.
5.
6.
7.
8.
9.
10.

Spelling Test 4

1.
2.
3.
4.
5.
6.
7.
8.
9.
10.

Spelling Test 5

1.
2.
3.
4.
5.
6.
7.
8.
9.
10.

Spelling Test 6

1.
2.
3.
4.
5.
6.
7.
8.
9.
10.

Spellings

Spelling Test 7

1.
2.
3.
4.
5.
6.
7.
8.
9.
10.

Spelling Test 8

1.
2.
3.
4.
5.
6.
7.
8.
9.
10.

Spelling Test 9

1.
2.
3.
4.
5.
6.
7.
8.
9.
10.

Spelling Test 10

1.
2.
3.
4.
5.
6.
7.
8.
9.
10.

Spelling Test 11

1.
2.
3.
4.
5.
6.
7.
8.
9.
10.

Spelling Test 12

1.
2.
3.
4.
5.
6.
7.
8.
9.
10.

Spellings

Spelling Test 13

1.
2.
3.
4.
5.
6.
7.
8.
9.
10.

Spelling Test 14

1.
2.
3.
4.
5.
6.
7.
8.
9.
10.

Spelling Test 15

1.
2.
3.
4.
5.
6.
7.
8.
9.
10.

Spelling Test 16

1.
2.
3.
4.
5.
6.
7.
8.
9.
10.

Spelling Test 17

1.
2.
3.
4.
5.
6.
7.
8.
9.
10.

Spelling Test 18

1.
2.
3.
4.
5.
6.
7.
8.
9.
10.

Spellings

Spelling Test 19	Spelling Test 20	Spelling Test 21
1.	1.	1.
2.	2.	2.
3.	3.	3.
4.	4.	4.
5.	5.	5.
6.	6.	6.
7.	7.	7.
8.	8.	8.
9.	9.	9.
10.	10.	10.

Spelling Test 22	Spelling Test 23	Spelling Test 24
1.	1.	1.
2.	2.	2.
3.	3.	3.
4.	4.	4.
5.	5.	5.
6.	6.	6.
7.	7.	7.
8.	8.	8.
9.	9.	9.
10.	10.	10.

Spellings

Spelling Test 25
1.
2.
3.
4.
5.
6.
7.
8.
9.
10.

Spelling Test 26
1.
2.
3.
4.
5.
6.
7.
8.
9.
10.

Spelling Test 27
1.
2.
3.
4.
5.
6.
7.
8.
9.
10.

Spelling Test 28
1.
2.
3.
4.
5.
6.
7.
8.
9.
10.

Spelling Test 29
1.
2.
3.
4.
5.
6.
7.
8.
9.
10.

Spelling Test 30
1.
2.
3.
4.
5.
6.
7.
8.
9.
10.

Spellings

Spelling Test 31	Spelling Test 32	Spelling Test 33
1.	1.	1.
2.	2.	2.
3.	3.	3.
4.	4.	4.
5.	5.	5.
6.	6.	6.
7.	7.	7.
8.	8.	8.
9.	9.	9.
10.	10.	10.

Spelling Test 34	Spelling Test 35	Spelling Test 36
1.	1.	1.
2.	2.	2.
3.	3.	3.
4.	4.	4.
5.	5.	5.
6.	6.	6.
7.	7.	7.
8.	8.	8.
9.	9.	9.
10.	10.	10.